JASON MRAZ MR. A-Z

This book was approved by Jason Mraz

Piano/Vocal arrangements by John Nicholas

Cherry Lane Music Company
Director of Publications/Project Editor: Mark Phillips
Publications Coordinator: Gabrielle Fastman

ISBN 1-57560-855-3

Visit our website at www.cherrylane.com

Jason Mraz
Talks About *MR. A-Z*

MR. A-Z is my pseudo-self-titled second album.

It definitely sounds like a sequel to my first album, *Waiting for My Rocket to Come*, only this time I used a slightly different octane of rocket fuel and had a greater amount of time to prepare its launch. Though I've collaborated with both my touring band and people whose influences have always affected my musical ear—such as my producer, Steve Lillywhite—this album is all Mraz from beginning to end, from alpha to omega, from the frontal lobe to the reptilian membrane…from A to Z. Thus I've assigned it the nomenclature it naturally desired and deserved: *MR. A-Z*.

MR. A-Z is 365 days of Mraz in just under an hour. The album took exactly a year to make, from the day the first word was scripted in January 2004 to mastering in January 2005, giving the whole affair a true four-season feel. These 12 songs recognize the events of my last few years, in which I left the coffeehouses where I was raised and was thrust into the theatre and arena circuit with the success of "Remedy." I'm pretty sure this album will please audiences from my caffeinated roots as well as those from my recently discovered Red Bull-and-beer-chugging jam band scene.

While the reality-based, tongue-in-cheek wordsmith of *Rocket* is back again, I also wanted this album to suggest that I was ready to reveal a little more about myself. The stories within these songs find your humble King of Denial having a go at my own placement in relationships lost and found again, in the ever-changing music business, as a geek and an artist and a smoker.

One of my goals was to allow my wisdom and perspective to resonate through a humorous persona that until now I'd used only in the live experience. A song like "Wordplay" is one of many born as a joke, meaning the writing exercise was full of laughs and great fun while it was being created. It is the first single and is meant to sound exactly as such. It's a straight satire on what a first single should sound like. Once you get past the initial shock of the song's pop velocity, you'll find a soft center composed by a happy little boy making a masterful mockery of his own agenda, beating the average critic to the punch, if I do say so myself.

MR. A-Z is the first time I've dared to actually consider myself a "recording artist," having gained a better understanding of the overall process through the experience. The primary musical objective for the album was to paint my vocals over backdrops that best reflected the nature of each individual song, to showcase my character over a variety of beautiful multi-genre grooves and styles and soundscapes. *Rocket* faintly touched upon a similar idea, but this time it's led to something truly different, with some sounds that I consider to be a new kind of music altogether.

I should note that Steve Lillywhite's work on this album had a tremendous influence on my writing and on the way we came to arrange and play the songs. Steve is so unconventional in his method of recording and producing. He goes into each album he produces with no preconceptions whatsoever. In a sense, he became a member of the band, adding an experienced ear and voice to our thought processes. He knows how to bring the best out of the players and capture a solid live take that becomes the belly of the track.

Those bellies were recorded at Allaire Studios near Woodstock, New York, and then tinkered with at my home studio in San Diego. "Clockwatching" was the first song we all knew would be on the record—it was Steve's favorite from the get-go—so of course it wound up being the most difficult one to record.

Dennis (a.k.a. "the Merch Guy"), my friend Scottish songwriter Ainslie Henderson, and I wrote "Clockwatching" together on a retreat in Wyoming about a year before we made the record. We did the whole thing with programmed beats and vocal delays, making it a fun sonic tribute to the Cure and other '80s sound-alikes. I composed the words on top of a washing machine in our quaint Cody cabin, culling bits from an assortment of scrapbook raps and fresh ideas from my San Diego to Wyoming drive.

The final product has the coolest rhythm track on the album, I think, with my drummer Adam King translating the original techno groove by playing like a machine. It swings between '80s grooves and bright beats, stopping and starting in the most peculiar places. That's a little something we learned from our travels with the Dave Matthews Band—audiences think you're great if you can stop and start at the same time.

I could go on and on about every last tune on *MR. A-Z*, like how "Life Is Wonderful" started as a soft-core song called "Crane," then how, inspired by the electronica duo Zero 7, Steve and I morphed it into something more simmering and psychedelic. But I think that I probably shouldn't go into too much detail about each song. Over the course of recording *MR. A-Z*, Steve taught me many things that will resonate throughout my recording career. But there was one particular thing that makes a lot of sense in this current scenario: "An artist should never have to explain what the songs are about," he said. "The listeners will determine that for themselves."

Let's just say that, taken collectively, the songs on *MR. A-Z* represent a specific time in my life. After all, a recording is ultimately a record of an event that took place only once. Thus, *Rocket* had a freshman's perspective on life and love—admittedly with a bit of an unabashed know-it-all mentality. On *MR. A-Z* I'm posing as the more appropriate sophomore, unafraid to admit my mistakes, good-natured in my verbal attacks, yet still hanging on to enough of that sophomoric angle to avoid playing it safe. This is most certainly an album that I can happily put on my application as I approach my graduation…

—Jason Mraz
May 2005

Life Is Wonderful

Words and Music by
Jason Mraz

Moderately fast

It takes a crane to build _____ a crane.
_____ a word,

It takes two floors _____ to make a _____ sto- ry.
and it takes some words _____ to make an _____ ac- tion.

It takes an egg _____ to make a hen. _____ It takes a hen _____ to make an egg. _____
And it takes some work _____ to make it work. _____ It takes some good _____ to make it hurt. _____

*Recorded a half step lower.

Fm

C

There is no end to what I'm _____ say - ing.
It takes some bad for sat - is - fac - tion.

|1.
G

Tacet

It takes a thought to make ___

|2.
G

Am

Ah, la, la, la, la, la, la. Life ___

Dm

G

C

___ is won - der - ful. ___ Ah, la, la, la, la, la, la. Life ___ goes full cir - cle.

Am

Dm

G

Ah, la, la, la, la. Life ___ is won - der - ful. ___ Ah, la, la, la, la. ___

young. It takes some cold to know the sun. It takes the one to have

the oth - er. _____ And it takes no time to fall in

love. _____ But it ____ takes you ___ years ____ to

know what love _____ is. And it takes some fears to make you

trust. It takes those tears to make it rust. ____ It takes the dust ____ to have it pol-

ished. ____ Yeah. ____ Ah, la, ____ la, la, la, la. Life ____

____ is wonder-ful. ____ Ah, ____ la, la, la, la, la. Life ____

____ goes full cir-cle. ____ Ah, la, la, la, la, la. Life ____

11

Repeat and fade

Wordplay

Words and Music by
Jason Mraz and Kevin Kadish

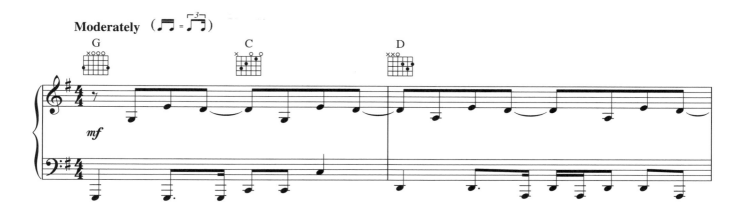

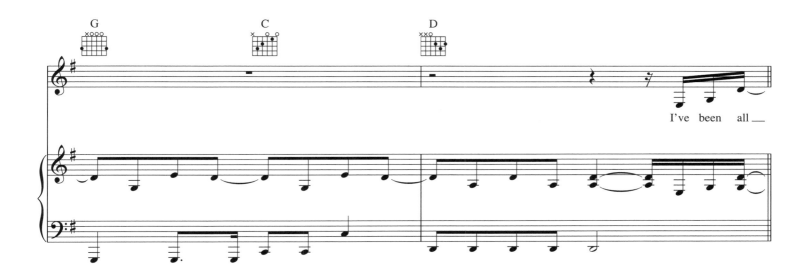

I've been all

_____ a - round the world. I've _____ been a new sen - sa - tion. But it

_____ I got your rem - e - dy. For those who don't re - mem - ber me, well,

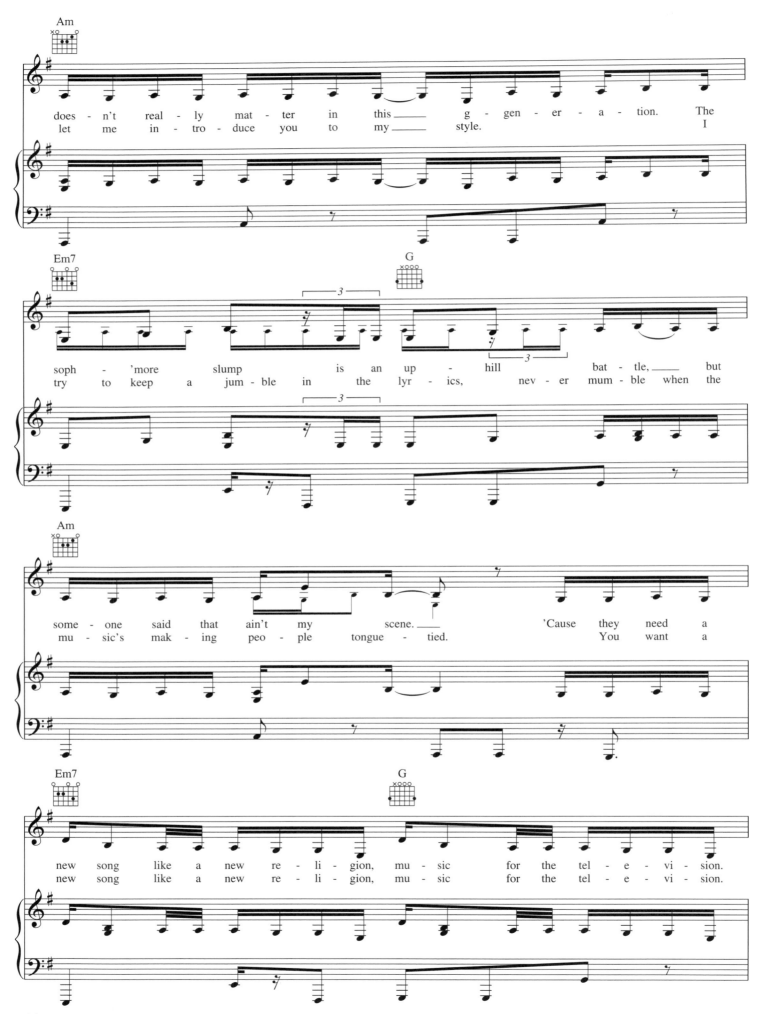

Am

I can't do the long di - vi - sion. Some - one do the math ____ 'fore the
I can't do the long di - vi - sion. Some - one do the math ____ 'fore the

Em7   **G**

rec - ord la - bel puts me on a shelf up in the freez - er.
peo - ple write me off like I'm a one - hit won - der.

Am

Got - ta find an - oth - er way to live the life of lei - sure. So I
Got - ta find an - oth - er way to keep from go - ing un - der. Pull

Em   **G**   **Am7**

drop my top, mix and I min - gle. Is ev - 'ry - bod - y read - y for the sin - gle? And it goes:
out the stops. Got your at - ten - tion. I guess it's time a - gain for me to men - tion the word - play.

15

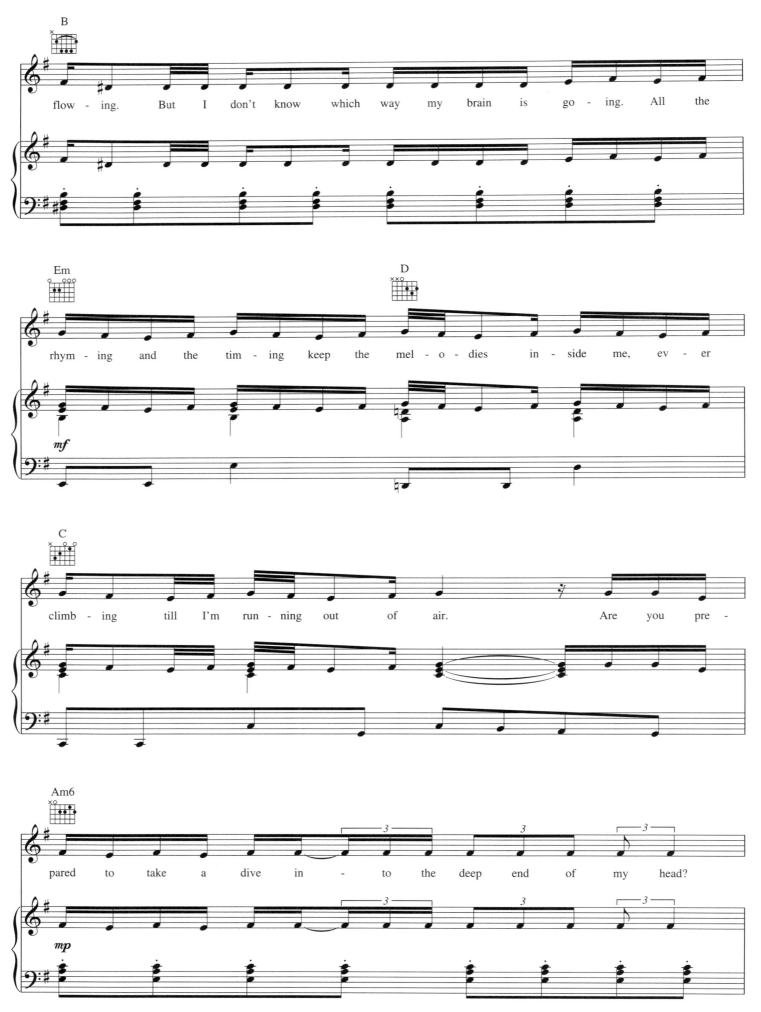

Geek in the Pink

Words and Music by
Jason Mraz, Kevin Kadish,
Scott Storch and Ian Sheridan

*Recorded a half step lower.

lis - ten to this.____ Don't wan - na miss it while it's hit - tin'.
eye - ing me down ____ like al - read - y a bad boy - friend.

Some - times ____ you got - ta fit in to get in, but
Well, she can get her toys out of the drawer, then. 'Cause

don't ev - er quit 'cause soon I'm gon - na let you in. Well, see, }
I ain't com - in' home. I don't need that at - ten - tion. See, }

I don't care what you might think a - bout ____ me. { 1.3. You'll get
{ 2. She'll get

Did You Get My Message?

Words and Music by
Jason Mraz and Dan Wilson

Did you

get my mes- sage, the one I left?__ Well, I was try- ing to con- dense ev- 'ry- thing__ that I meant__ in a

*Recorded a half step lower.

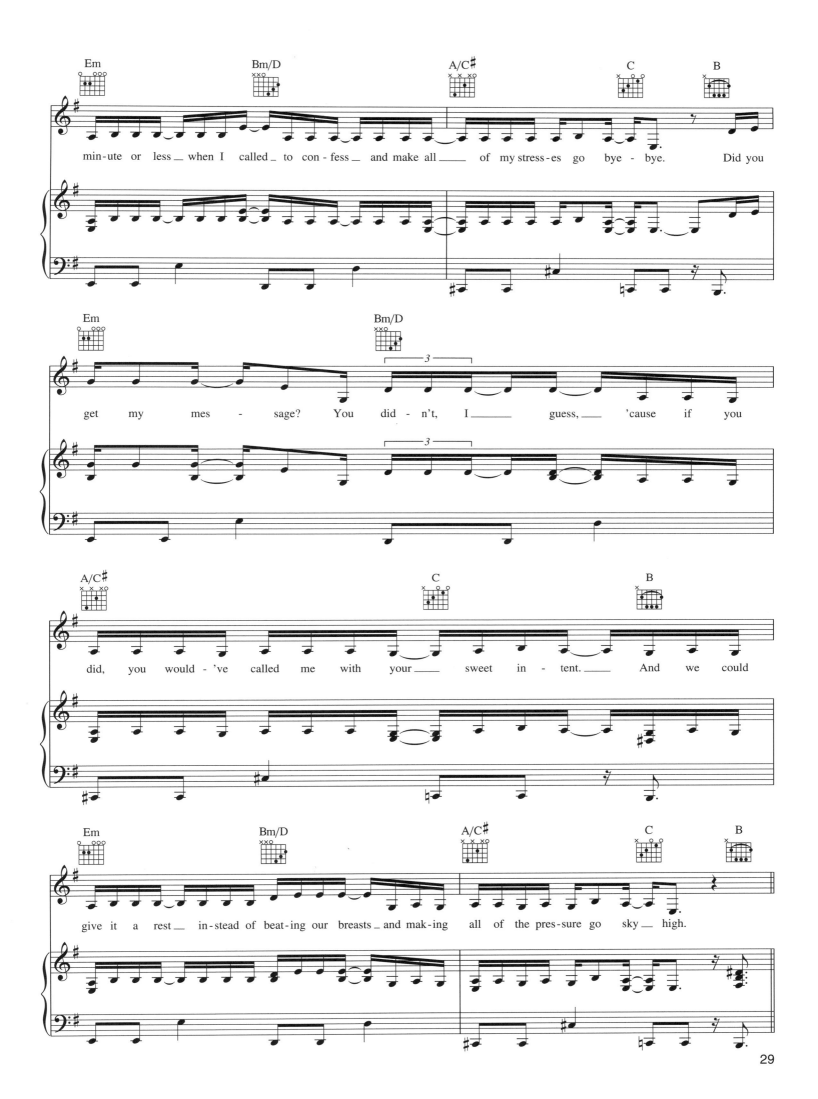

D.S. al Coda I

32

Mr. Curiosity

Words and Music by
Jason Mraz, Lester Mendez and Dennis Morris

find _____ me, find me.) _____

D.S. al Coda

Cu - ri - ous - i - ty, ___ be Mis - ter Please ___ Do Come And Find Me. ___ Love is

Clockwatching

Words and Music by
Jason Mraz, Dennis Morris
and Ainslie Henderson

Lady dreamer, you might be the sound-

est sleep-er. To-night, sleep tight and

build your nest up-on my shoul-der.

Bella Luna

Words and Music by
Jason Mraz and William Galewood

Moderately fast (Latin feel)

Mys-ter-y, the moon, _____ a hole _____ in _____ the sky, _____

a su-per-nat-'ral night-light, _____ so full _____ but of-ten wry. _____ A pair of eyes, _____ a clos-ing _____ one, _____ _____ a cho-sen child of gold-en sun. _____ A mar-ble dog _____ that chas-es cars to far-thest reach-es of the beach _____ and far be-yond _____

Am
Bm7♭5

E
Am

You are ___ an il - lu - mi - nat - ing an - chor _____

Bm7♭5

___ of leagues too in - fi - nite in num - ber, _____ crash - ing

Am

waves ___ and break - ing thun - der, ___ tid - ing the ebb and flow ___ of hun - ger. ___

You're danc-ing na-ked there for me.___ You ex-pose all mem-o-ry. You make the most___ of bound-a-ry.___ You're the ghost___ of roy-al-ty im-pos-ing love. You are the queen and king com-bin-ing ev-'ry-thing,___ in-ter-twin-ing like a ring a-round___ the

finger of a girl. ___ I'm just a sing - er; you're the world. ___

___ All I can bring ya is the lan - guage of ___ a ___ lov -

er. ___ Bel - la Lu -

na - a - a, ___ my beau - ti - ful, beau - ti - ful

moon, _____ how you swoon _____ me like no oth - er, _____ oh. _____

ee - ee - ease, Bel - la, you _____ beau - ti - ful lu - na, _____

D.S. al Coda

oh, Bel - la, do what you _____ do. _____

Plane

Words and Music by
Jason Mraz and Dennis Morris

*Recorded a half step lower.

I can - not wait to call you and tell you that I land -
ed some - where and hand you a square ___ of the air - port
and walk you through the maze ___ of the map that I'm gaz - ing at, ___
grace - ful - ly un - named ___ and feel - ing guilt - y for the luck and the look that you gave ___ me. ___

If the plane goes down, damn.

You get me high - mind - ed.

You keep me high.

65

O, Lover

Words and Music by
Jason Mraz and Dennis Morris

Moderately fast

Bm

What's the worst thing that could hap - pen? We could change our minds.

Gm   F#m

That seems to be the hot - test top - ic at this time.

Bm

We sit - tin' a - round in med - i - ta - tion, drag - on chas - ing won - d'ring

Gm   F#m

who's hold - ing who's got the will to draw the line.

Oh, God on-ly knows __ our con-tra-dic-tions to quit-ting. It's a hate-

to-love __ re-la-tion-ship thing. __ A fi-re un-der you __ is so ful-fill-

ing. I feel there's noth-ing more. __ I'm giv-ing, giv-ing you __ the choke

hold. _____ My flirt-ing with dis-as-ter is mod-ern love. _____ Ooh, _____

76

ro - mance, __ 'cause __ when the week - end starts, the guilt - y par - ty's on. __

Week - end   par - ty's   o - ver.
Week - end   par - ty's   o - ver.
Week - end   par - ty's   o - ver.
Week - end   par - ty's   o - ver.

Don't   stop;   let's   get   clos - er.   Fri - day   got   cold   shoul - der.
Don't   stop;   let's   get   low - er   I   won't   blow   your   cov - er.
Don't   stop;   let's   get   clos - er.   Fri - day   was   me - di - o - cre.
Don't   stop;   let's   sup - pose   a   I   won't   blow   your   cov - er.

|1.2.3.| |4.|

Mon - day   got   a   new   com - po - sure.   Op - por - tu - nis - tic   lov - er.
Op - por - tu - nis - tic   lov - er.
Mon - day   I'm   self - ex - posed,   uh?

Please Don't Tell Her

Words and Music by
Jason Mraz and Eric Hinojosa

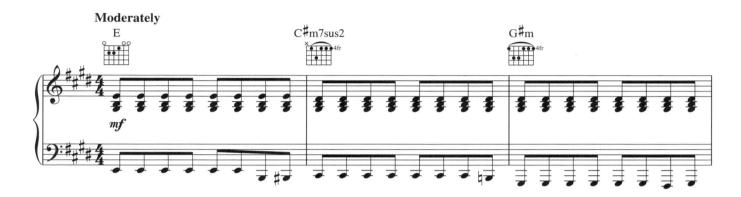

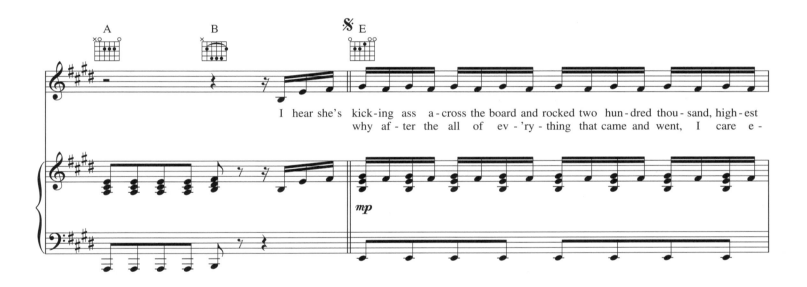

I hear she's kick-ing ass a-cross the board and rocked two hun-dred thou-sand, high-est
why af-ter the all of ev-'ry-thing that came and went, I care e-

score, and just in time to save the world of be-ing tak-en o-ver. ___ She's a war-
nough to still be sing-ing of the bit-ter end and bro-ken e-ras. ___ I told ___

Please __ don't tell her that I've been mean-ing to

miss __ her, be-cause I __ don't. __

She was the

girl with the broad-est shoul-ders. But she would die __ be-fore I crawled o-ver __ them. __

She is tall-er than I am. ____ She knew I would-n't mind the view ____ there, or the al-ti-tude ____ with a mouth-ful of air. She let me down; ____ the doubt ____ came out _____ un-til the now _____ be-came lat-er. Say that it is-n't so, how she eas-i-ly come, ____

how she eas-y go. _____ Please __ don't

tell her 'cause she don't real - ly ___ need to know _____

that I'm cra - zy like ____ the rest ___

of us. _____ And I'm

The Forecast

Words and Music by
Jason Mraz and Eric Hinojosa

one might find me fool-ish to not be count-ing on the sun. ___ But your

mouth is ___ my um-brel-la now, and I'm hold-ing ___ your tongue. ___ And if the

rains should ___ pour, ___ for sure ___ with you ___ I'll ___ be, ___ ee. ___

___ And cra-zy is the fore - cast ___ all ___ week. ___

man, _____ but you are light - ning ___ strik - ing. _____

_____ La, la, la.

Here comes __ the sun _____ and the rain.

D.S. al Coda

All at once ___ now they __ sing. __

Song for a Friend

Words and Music by
Jason Mraz, Eric Hinojosa,
Dennis Morris and Dan Wilson

"Well, you're mag - ic," he said, but don't let it all go to your head, 'cause I bet if you all ___ had it all fig - ured out, ___ then you'd

He said that you've got to love _____ your - self. ____

He said you should - n't mum - ble when __ you speak, __ but keep your tongue __

____ up in __ your __ cheek. ____ And if you stum - ble on - to some - thing bet - ter, re - mem - ber that it's

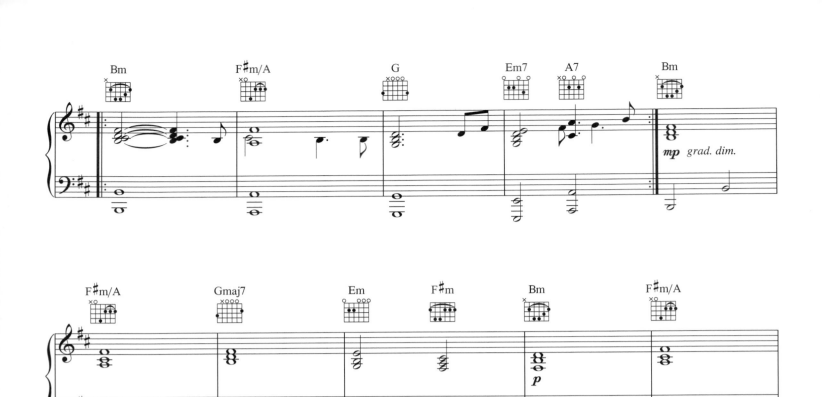

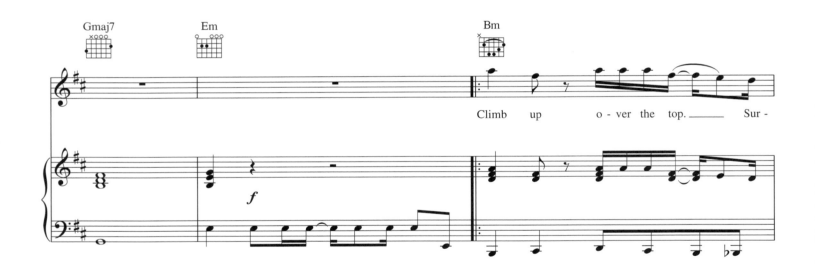

Climb up over the top._____ Sur-

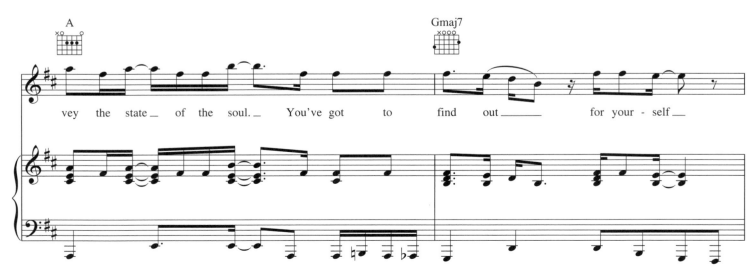

vey the state __ of the soul. __ You've got to find out _____ for your-self __

wheth - er or not __ you're tru - ly try - ing. Why not give it a shot? _____

Shake it; take __ con - trol, __ in - ev - i - ta - bly wind up __ find - ing for your - self __ all the strengths __

Play 3 times

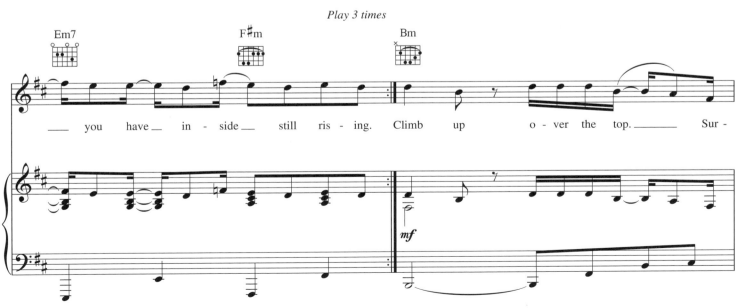

____ you have __ in - side __ still ris - ing. Climb up o - ver the top. _____ Sur -

More Great Piano/Vocal Books
FROM CHERRY LANE

For a complete listing of Cherry Lane titles available,
including contents listings, please visit our web site at

www.cherrylane.com

See your local music dealer or contact:

CHERRY LANE
MUSIC COMPANY
6 East 32nd Street, New York, NY 10016

Quality in Printed Music

EXCLUSIVELY DISTRIBUTED BY

HAL•LEONARD®
CORPORATION
7777 W. BLUEMOUND RD. P.O. BOX 13819 MILWAUKEE, WI 53213

Prices, contents and availability subject to change without notice.

0404

More Big-Note & Easy Piano Books

For a complete listing of Cherry Lane titles available, including contents listings, please visit our web site at www.cherrylane.com

CLASSICAL CHRISTMAS
Easy solo arrangements of 30 wonderful holiday songs: Ave Maria • Dance of the Sugar Plum Fairy • Evening Prayer • Gesu Bambino • Hallelujah! • He Shall Feed His Flock • March of the Toys • O Come, All Ye Faithful • O Holy Night • Pastoral Symphony • Sheep May Safely Graze • Sinfonia • Waltz of the Flowers • and more.
___02500112 Easy Piano Solo $9.95

BEST OF JOHN DENVER
___02505512 Easy Piano $9.95

DOWN THE AISLE
Easy piano arrangements of 20 beloved pop and classical wedding songs, including: Air on the G String • Ave Maria • Canon in D • Follow Me • Give Me Forever (I Do) • Jesu, Joy of Man's Desiring • Prince of Denmark's March • Through the Years • Trumpet Tune • Unchained Melody • Wedding March • When I Fall in Love • You Decorated My Life • and more.
___025000267 Easy Piano $9.95

EASY BROADWAY SHOWSTOPPERS
Easy piano arrangements of 16 traditional and new Broadway standards, including: "Impossible Dream" from *Man of La Mancha* • "Unusual Way" from *Nine* • "This Is the Moment" from *Jekyll & Hyde* • many more.
___02505517 Easy Piano $12.95

GOLD AND GLORY –
THE ROAD TO EL DORADO
This beautiful souvenir songbook features full-color photos and 8 songs from the DreamWorks animated film. Includes original songs by Elton John and Tim Rice, and a score by Hans Zimmer and John Powell. Songs: Cheldorado – Score • El Dorado • Friends Never Say Goodbye • It's Tough to Be a God • Someday out of the Blue (Theme from El Dorado) • The Trail We Blaze • Without Question • Wonders of the New World: To Shibalba.
___02500274 Easy Piano $14.95

A FAMILY CHRISTMAS AROUND
THE PIANO
25 songs for hours of family fun, including: Away in a Manger • Deck the Hall • The First Noel • God Rest Ye Merry, Gentlemen • Hark! the Herald Angels Sing • Jingle Bells • Jolly Old St. Nicholas • Joy to the World • O Little Town of Bethlehem • Silent Night, Holy Night • The Twelve Days of Christmas • and more.
___02500398 Easy Piano $7.95

GILBERT & SULLIVAN FOR EASY PIANO
20 great songs from 6 great shows by this beloved duo renowned for their comedic classics. Includes: Behold the Lord High Executioner • The Flowers That Bloom in the Spring • He Is an Englishman • I Am the Captain of the Pinafore • (I'm Called) Little Buttercup • Miya Sama • Three Little Maids • Tit-Willow • We Sail the Ocean Blue • When a Merry Maiden Marries • When Britain Really Ruled the Waves • When Frederic Was a Lad • and more.
___02500270 Easy Piano $12.95

GREAT CONTEMPORARY BALLADS
___02500150 Easy Piano $12.95

HOLY CHRISTMAS CAROLS
COLORING BOOK
A terrific songbook with 7 sacred carols and lots of coloring pages for the young pianist. Songs include: Angels We Have Heard on High • The First Noel • Hark! The Herald Angels Sing • It Came upon a Midnight Clear • O Come All Ye Faithful • O Little Town of Bethlehem • Silent Night.
___02500277 Five-Finger Piano $6.95

JEKYLL & HYDE – VOCAL SELECTIONS
Ten songs from the Wildhorn/Bricusse Broadway smash, arranged for big-note: In His Eyes • It's a Dangerous Game • Lost in the Darkness • A New Life • No One Knows Who I Am • Once Upon a Dream • Someone Like You • Sympathy, Tenderness • Take Me as I Am • This Is the Moment.
___02505515 Easy Piano $12.95
___02500023 Big-Note Piano $9.95

JUST FOR KIDS – NOT!
CHRISTMAS SONGS
This unique collection of 14 Christmas favorites is fun for the whole family! Kids can play the full-sounding big-note solos alone, or with their parents (or teachers) playing accompaniment for the thrill of four-hand piano! Includes: Deck the Halls • Jingle Bells • Silent Night • What Child Is This? • and more.
___02505510 Big-Note Piano $7.95

JUST FOR KIDS – NOT! CLASSICS
Features big-note arrangements of classical masterpieces, plus optional accompaniment for adults. Songs: Air on the G String • Dance of the Sugar Plum Fairy • Für Elise • Jesu, Joy of Man's Desiring • Ode to Joy • Pomp and Circumstance • The Sorcerer's Apprentice • William Tell Overture • and more!
___02505513 Classics....................$7.95
___02500301 More Classics $7.95

JUST FOR KIDS – NOT! FUN SONGS
Fun favorites for kids everywhere in big-note arrangements for piano, including: Bingo • Eensy Weensy Spider • Farmer in the Dell • Jingle Bells • London Bridge • Pop Goes the Weasel • Puff the Magic Dragon • Skip to My Lou • Twinkle, Twinkle Little Star • and more!
___02505523 Fun Songs.................$7.95
___02505528 More Fun Songs $7.95

JUST FOR KIDS – NOT!
TV THEMES & MOVIE SONGS
Entice the kids to the piano with this delightful collection of songs and themes from movies and TV. These big-note arrangements include themes from The Brady Bunch and The Addams Family, as well as Do-Re-Mi (The Sound of Music), theme from Beetlejuice (Day-O) and Puff the Magic Dragon. Each song includes an accompaniment part for teacher or adult so that the kids can experience the joy of four-hand playing as well! Plus performance tips.
___02505507 TV Themes & Movie
               Songs $9.95
___02500304 More TV Themes & Movie
               Songs $9.95

LOVE BALLADS
___02500152 EZ-Play Today #364 $7.95

MERRY CHRISTMAS, EVERYONE
Over 20 contemporary and classic all-time holiday favorites arranged for big-note piano or easy piano. Includes: Away in a Manger • Christmas Like a Lullaby • The First Noel • Joy to the World • The Marvelous Toy • and more.
___02505600 Big-Note Piano $9.95

See your local music
dealer or contact:

CHERRY LANE
MUSIC COMPANY
6 East 32nd Street, New York, NY 10016

EXCLUSIVELY DISTRIBUTED BY

HAL•LEONARD®
7777 W. BLUEMOUND RD. P.O. BOX 13819 MILWAUKEE, WI 53213

POKEMON 2 B.A. MASTER
This great songbook features easy piano arrangements of 13 tunes from the hit TV series: 2.B.A. Master • Double Trouble (Team Rocket) • Everything Changes • Misty's Song • My Best Friends • Pokémon (Dance Mix) • Pokémon Theme • PokéRAP • The Time Has Come (Pikachu's Goodbye) • Together, Forever • Viridian City • What Kind of Pokémon Are You? • You Can Do It (If You Really Try). Includes a full-color, 8-page pull-out section featuring characters and scenes from this super hot show.
___02500145 Easy Piano $12.95

POKEMON
Five-finger arrangements of 7 songs from the hottest show for kids! Includes: Pokémon Theme • The Time Has Come (Pikachu's Goodbye) • 2B A Master • Together, Forever • What Kind of Pokémon Are You? • You Can Do It (If You Really Try). Also features cool character artwork, and a special section listing the complete lyrics for the "PokéRAP."
___02500291 Five-Finger Piano $7.95

POP/ROCK HITS
___02500153 E-Z Play Today #366 $7.95

POP/ROCK LOVE SONGS
Easy arrangements of 18 romatic favorites, including: Always • Bed of Roses • Butterfly Kisses • Follow Me • From This Moment On • Hard Habit to Break • Leaving on a Jet Plane • When You Say Nothing at All • more.
___02500151 Easy Piano $10.95

POPULAR CHRISTMAS CAROLS
COLORING BOOK
Kids are sure to love this fun holiday songbook! It features five-finger piano arrangements of seven Christmas classics, complete with coloring pages throughout! Songs include: Deck the Hall • Good King Wenceslas • Jingle Bells • Jolly Old St. Nicholas • O Christmas Tree • Up on the Housetop • We Wish You a Merry Christmas.
___02500276 Five-Finger Piano $6.95

PUFF THE MAGIC DRAGON & 54 OTHER
ALL-TIME CHILDREN'S FAVORITE
SONGS
55 timeless songs enjoyed by generations of kids, and sure to be favorites for years to come. Songs include: A-Tisket A-Tasket • Alouette • Eensy Weensy Spider • The Farmer in the Dell • I've Been Working on the Railroad • If You're Happy and You Know It • Joy to the World • Michael Finnegan • Oh Where, Oh Where Has My Little Dog Gone • Silent Night • Skip to My Lou • This Old Man • and many more.
___02500017 Big-Note Piano $12.95

PURE ROMANCE
___02500268 Easy Piano $10.95

SCHOOLHOUSE ROCK SONGBOOK
10 unforgettable songs from the classic television educational series, now experiencing a booming resurgence in popularity from Generation X'ers to today's kids! Includes: I'm Just a Bill • Conjunction Junction • Lolly, Lolly, Lolly (Get Your Adverbs Here) • The Great American Melting Pot • and more.
___02505576 Big-Note Piano $8.95

BEST OF JOHN TESH
___02505511 Easy Piano $12.95
___02500128 E-Z Play Today #356 $8.95

TOP COUNTRY HITS
___02500154 E-Z Play Today #365 $7.95